VOLUME 1

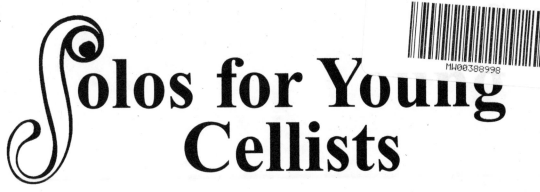

Solos for Young Cellists

Compiled, Edited, Arranged and Composed by Cellist **Carey Cheney**

Art Design: Ernesto Ebanks
Cover Photo: Cello by Paul Schuback, Schuback Violin Shop,
Portland, Oregon, 1986; owned by Carey Cheney
Photo Credit: Elliott W. Cheney

© 2003 Summy-Birchard Music
division of Summy-Birchard Inc.
Exclusive print rights administered by Alfred Music Publishing Co., Inc.
All Rights Reserved   Printed in USA
ISBN 1-58951-208-1

Contents

Simple Folk Songs 6

  1. Frère Jacques (Pattern One) 6

  2. Brahms' Lullaby 7

  3. The Little Fiddle 8

  4. Swedish Folk Song 9

  5. Frère Jacques (Pattern Four) 10

  6. Entre le Bœuf et L'Ane Gris 11

  7. The Nut-Tree 12

  8. Song of Thanksgiving 13

Scherzo, Op. 12, No. 3 . . . . *H. Schlemuller* 14

Forward, March!, Op. 14, No. 6 . . . . *H. Schlemuller* 17

Livi's Blues . . . . *E. W. Cheney* 24

Fairytales (L'Innocence) . . . . *W. H. Squire* 27

Clock Tower Bells . . . . *C. Cheney* 32

Budapesto . . . . *C. Cheney* 34

Gondola Song . . . . *H. Schlemuller* 36

Concerto in C Major, F. III., No. 6* . . . . *A. Vivaldi*

  Allegro 43

  Largo 49

  Allegro 50

*Realizations of orchestral reductions by David Dunford.

INTRODUCTION

Solos for Young Cellists is an eight-volume series of music compilations with companion CDs. This series is not designed as a method, but rather as a collection of wonderful music. This collection offers young cellists the opportunity to work in various positions, techniques, meters, keys and musical styles. These pieces provide exciting and diverse additions to the current repertoire. Many of the works in the collection are recognized as major repertoire pieces while others are newly published or original compositions. Compiled, edited and recorded by Carey Cheney, *Solos for Young Cellists* is a graded series of works ranging from elementary to advanced levels and represents a truly exciting variety of musical genres and techniques. The collection will become a valuable resource for teachers and students of all ages and levels. The piano track recorded on the second half of each CD gives the cellist the chance to practice performing with accompaniments up to tempo.

1. Frère Jacques

(Optional shift to 4th position indic. below)

French Folk Song

2. Lullaby

J. Brahms

3. The Little Fiddle

German Folk Song

4. Swedish Folk Song

Traditional

5. Frère Jacques
Pattern Four

French Folk Song

6. Entre le Boeuf et L'Ane Gris
(Between the Ox and the Gray Donkey)

French Canadian Folk Song

7. The Nut-Tree

Old English Song

8. Song of Thanksgiving

E. Kremser

Scherzo
Op.12, No. 3

Hugo Schlemuller

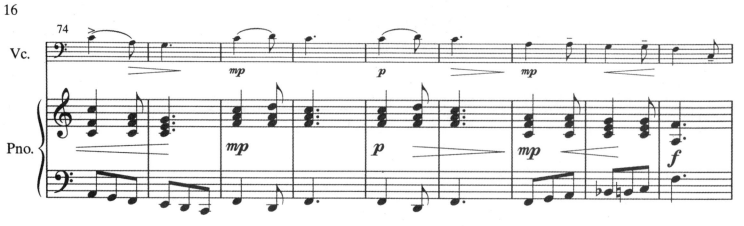

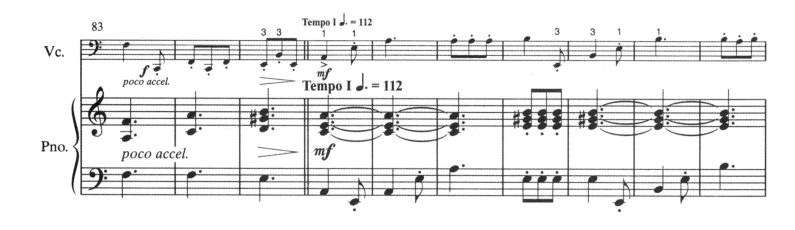

Forward, March!

Op. 14, No. 6

Hugo Schlemuller

18

20810

Livi's Blues

Elliott W. Cheney

1' 20"

THE TEACHER

The teacher is a professional whose principal function is to lead the students step by step in the art of string playing in such a manner that each individual play appears relatively simple and flows into the next. Her all-consuming goal is to open the doors of self-expression. Convinced that each person has something within him uniquely beautiful and individual just waiting to be freed, she realizes that she, as the teacher, does not create it—it already exists. Her role is to guide and help the student develop technical tools so that the internal beauty can flow freely.

The teacher looks on herself as a key-holder and recognizes that the ease with which a door is opened has nothing to do with the contents of the room and that untold splendors may lie behind the door with the most stubborn lock. And she believes the medium that her student has chosen for self-expression is one of the most beautiful and elemental of all—the vibrating string.

Excerpt from *Playing the String Game*
by Phyllis Young

Fairytales
L'Innocence

W.H. Squire

Clock Tower Bells

Carey Cheney

1' 00"

Budapesto

Carey Cheney

1' 01"

Gondola Song
Op. 14, No. 1

Hugo Schlemuller

38

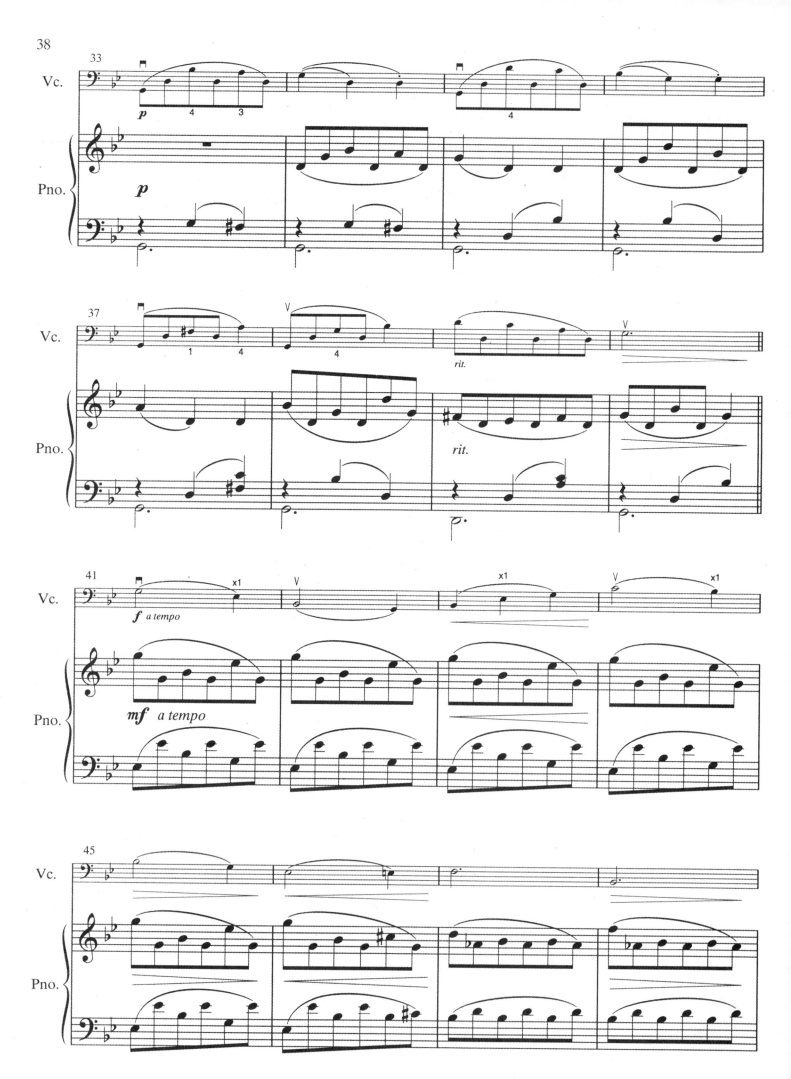

20810

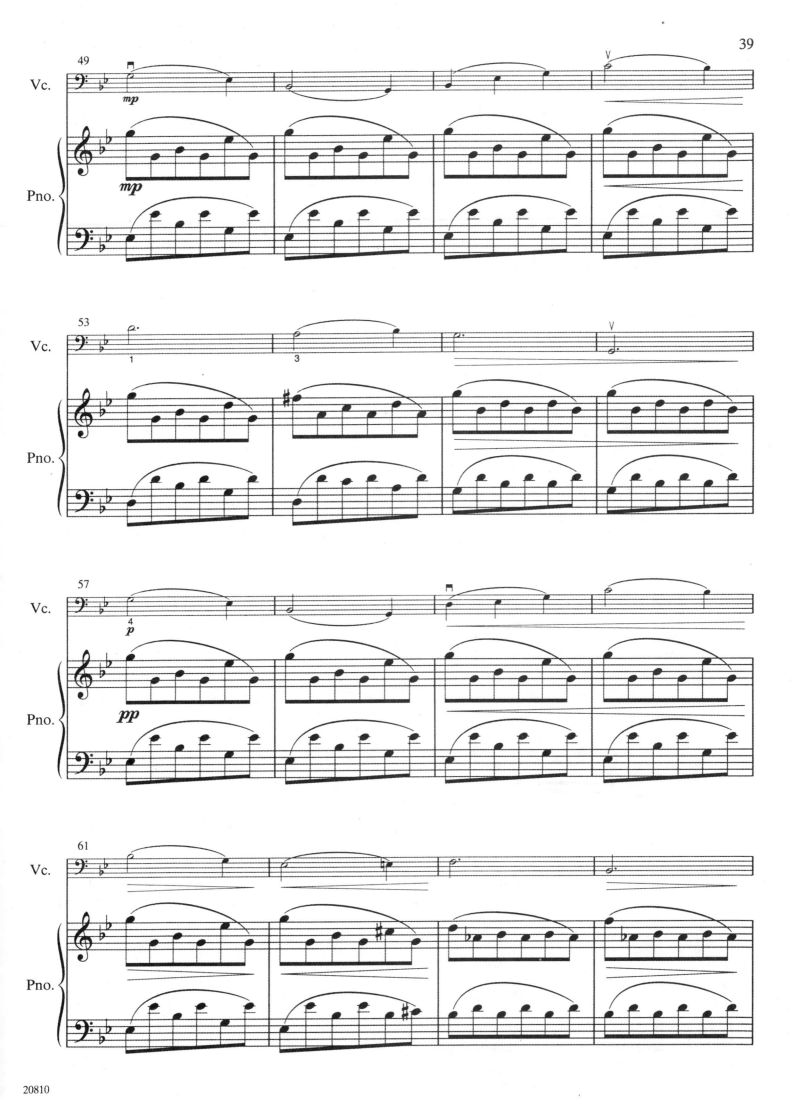

40

20810

Concerto in C Major
F. III, No. 6
(First movement)

A. Vivaldi

20810

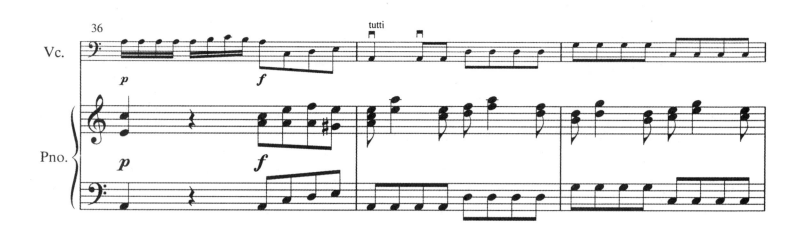

Concerto in C Major
F. III, No. 6
(Second movement)

A. Vivaldi

Concerto in C Major
F. III, No. 6
(Third movement)

A. Vivaldi

52

20810